Earth's Amazing Environments

Elizabeth Corfe

Contents

Amazing Environments

Earth is home to many amazing environments. Life is found nearly everywhere in these environments – in deserts, oceans, tropical rainforests and at the poles.

a herd of camels in the Judea desert, Israel

Yet some of these environments are in danger. This means that the plants and animals that live in these environments are in danger, too.

Antarctica

an anglerfish

One cause of this danger is from global warming. Global warming means the Earth is getting hotter. It is caused by too many **greenhouse gases** in Earth's **atmosphere**.

Global warming has happened because of things such as:

- too much **pollution**, from cars and factories
- cutting down too many forests.

Global warming is bad for us and for the animals and plants we share Earth with.

Read on to learn about Earth's amazing environments, why they are in danger – and what **you** can do to help.

Deserts

Deserts are the driest environments on Earth. It hardly ever rains in a desert and a desert can be hot or cold.

Antarctic desert

The word *desert* comes from the Latin word *desertum* which means "an **abandoned** place".

Earth's Deserts

There are ten large deserts on Earth.

Sahara desert

Desert Life

In hot deserts the sun is strong, and the ground is hot. These deserts seem empty ... but are they? Most hot deserts are full of life.

When the sun goes down, a hot desert can get very cold. Some can be 45°C in the day and drop to 0°C at night!

a scorpion

During the day, most desert animals hide from the sun. But as the sun goes down, the desert animals begin to stir.

Precious Water

Living things need water to **survive**. A desert is very dry so animals have to be clever at getting and storing water.

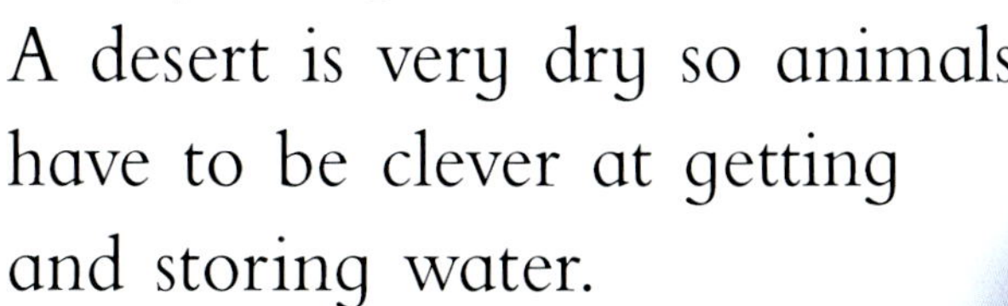

The Thorny devil lizard stores water in its thorns and skin.

The Fennec fox gets enough water from the flesh of the animals it eats.

A camel stores fat in its hump. The fat contains water.

Deserts in Danger

Global warming is putting Earth's deserts in danger. Some deserts are now hotter than they should be. Some are also drier than they should be. This is because less rain is falling in these deserts than it did before global warming.

Even small increases in temperature will threaten desert plants and animals.

With less water, desert plants and animals will no longer survive. Many may become **endangered** or even **extinct**.

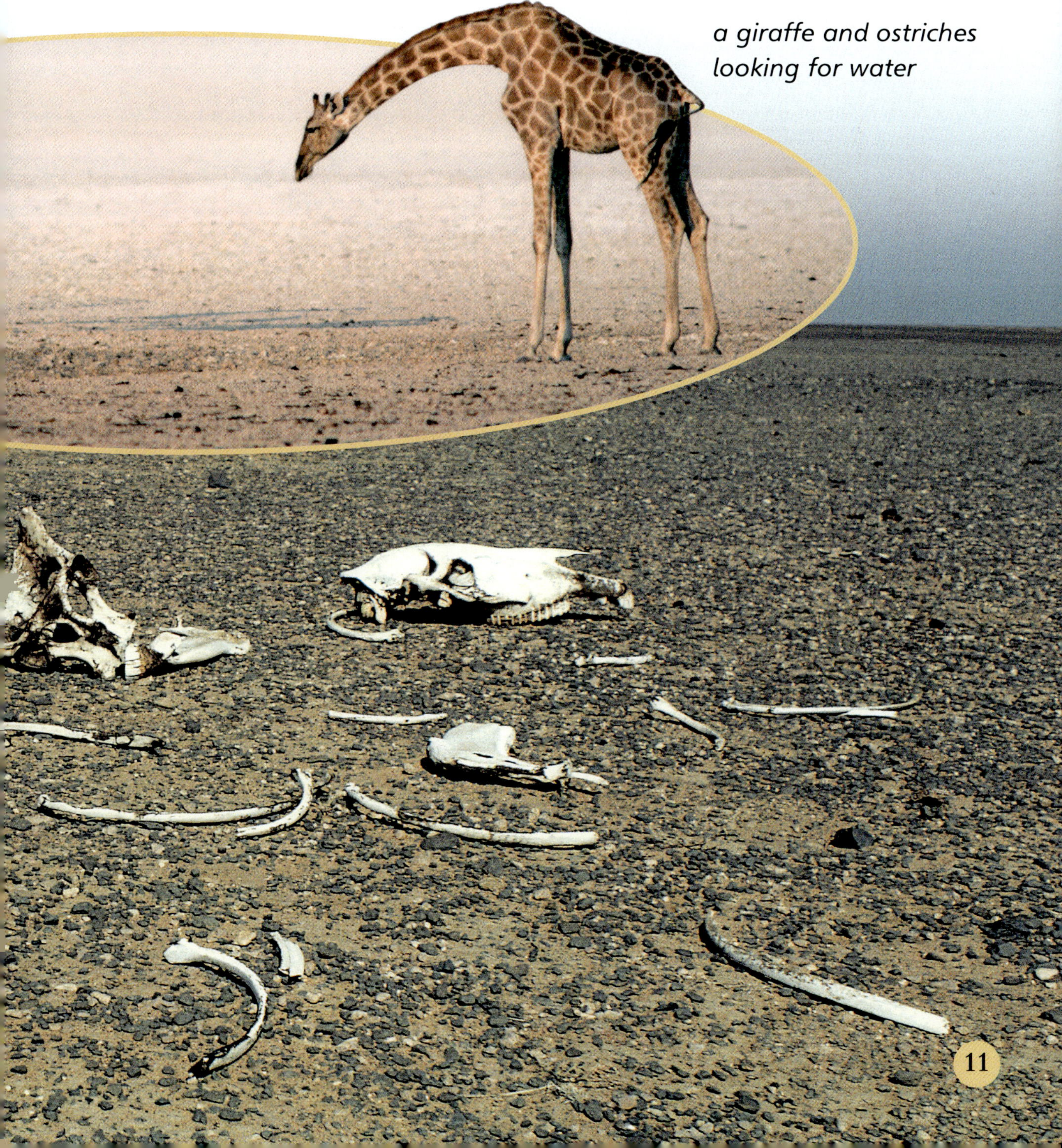

a giraffe and ostriches looking for water

Oceans

An ocean is a huge body of salt water. Oceans cover most of the Earth's **surface** – around 70%. That's over half of the Earth!

The smaller parts of oceans are called seas, gulfs, bays and straits.

More than half of Earth's oceans are over 3000 metres deep!

Earth's Oceans

There are five large oceans on Earth.

Ocean Life

Plants and animals of all shapes, sizes and colours live in the ocean. Even the deepest, darkest and coldest parts of Earth's oceans have life.

This is a Leafy Sea dragon, a type of seahorse. It looks like seaweed.

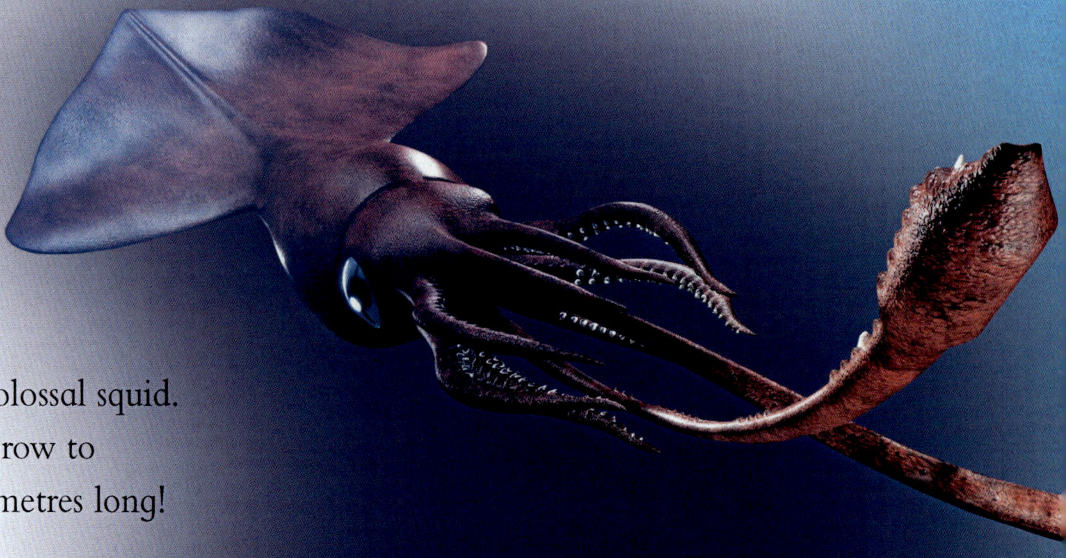

This is a Colossal squid. They can grow to around 14 metres long!

This is a blue whale.
It is the largest
animal on Earth!

This is an anglerfish.
It lives at the bottom
of the ocean.

Oceans in Danger

Global warming is making the oceans warmer, harming and even killing **marine** life.

Coral reefs are in danger. This is because the coral will die if the ocean is too warm for too long.

This coral, on the Great Barrier Reef in Australia, has died and turned white due to the ocean being too warm.

Marine animals such as whales will lose their food **supply**. Whales eat krill, and krill eat smaller ocean animals that may die due to global warming. So the krill will have no food, and the whales will have no food when the krill has gone.

a grey whale eating krill

Pollution such as oil spills can kill marine life. Animals, birds and fish can get covered in the oil and cannot stay warm, fly or swim.

a bird covered in oil from an oil spill

Tropical Rainforests

Tropical rainforests are very wet, warm forests. They are home to more than half of the Earth's animal and plant **species**!

The Amazon rainforest is the world's largest tropical rainforest.

Earth's Tropical Rainforests

The Earth's main tropical rainforests are found near the **equator**.

Chocolate, banana and mangoes all first grew in tropical rainforests. Today, they are grown on **plantations** in areas near tropical rainforests.

Rainforest Life

Tropical rainforests are filled with tall, leafy trees that make a kind of roof over the forest. The forest floor is very dark and wet. In between, there are smaller trees and plants.

The rainforest is filled with the sounds of animal, insect and bird life.

Colourful, beautiful and strange animals live in tropical rainforests.

The Queen Alexandra butterfly is the world's largest butterfly. It flies high up in the trees.

The Queen Alexandra butterfly is found in Papua New Guinea.

The orang-utan lives in the treetops. It sleeps in a nest made of leaves and branches.

The orang-utan is found in Sumatra and Borneo.

Rainforests in Danger

Global warming also harms rainforest plants and animals. As Earth becomes warmer, parts of a rainforest may die. Many animals that call these rainforests home will no longer have a place to live.

The Sumatran orang-utan is very endangered. This is because much of its rainforest home has been destroyed by human activities such as **logging**.

Earth's rainforests are also cut down for logging, **mining** and farming. This destroys many animals' **habitats**. Large numbers of rainforest animals have become endangered or extinct as a result.

In around 20 years time, over half of the Amazon rainforest will be gone. This is due to logging and clearing land for farming.

The Poles

There are two large icy environments on Earth that are both deserts. The Arctic is a huge area of ice covering the ocean around the North Pole. Antarctica is a huge area of ice that covers land around the South Pole.

a photo of Antarctica taken from space

The Arctic and Antarctica

The Arctic is in the northern **hemisphere**. Antarctica is in the southern hemisphere.

The North Pole is the northernmost point on Earth. The South Pole is the southernmost point on Earth.

Life on the Ice

Animals live in the Arctic and Antarctica. Most of the animals that live there have thick layers of fur, feathers or fat called blubber. Blubber keeps the animals warm.

emperor penguins, Antarctica

Polar bears live in the Arctic. They have thick fur and blubber to survive the cold. They **hibernate** during the really freezing weather.

Emperor penguins live in Antarctica. They have feathers and blubber to survive the cold. They also huddle together to keep warm.

Seals live in both **polar regions**. They have fur and thick blubber to survive the cold. They also hold their flippers against their bodies to keep warm.

a fur seal, Antarctica

Poles in Danger

Global warming is melting the ice in both the Arctic and Antarctica. Melting ice means animals that live in these environments will lose their habitats and **feeding grounds**.

Some scientists believe that within 100 years the polar bear will be extinct due to global warming.

Melting ice also means that ocean levels will rise, and may flood coastlines all over the world.

Adélie penguins, Antarctica

If Antarctica's ice melts, global ocean levels will rise by about 62 metres.

You Can Make a Difference!

Here are five things you can do to help care for and protect Earth's amazing environments.

Action!	Why It Helps
recycling	• less rubbish is made. • fewer trees will be logged. • less pollution will be caused. • will slow down global warming.
saving water	• all living things and environments need water to survive.
using less electricity	• less pollution will be released into the air. • will slow down global warming.
walking	• walking more and driving less means less pollution will be released into the air. • will slow down global warming.
talking!	• telling people will spread the word about how to protect Earth's amazing environments.

Glossary

abandoned
left empty; not lived in

atmosphere
the gases surrounding Earth

endangered
when a species is in danger of becoming extinct

equator
the imaginary line around the middle of Earth

extinct
when a species dies out

feeding grounds
places on land or in water where animals find food

greenhouse gases
polluting gases that trap heat in Earth's atmosphere

habitats
the environments that animals and plants live in

hemisphere
half of a sphere; Earth is a sphere so it has two hemispheres, the Northern hemisphere and the Southern hemisphere

hibernate
to pass the winter in an almost sleep-like state

logging
cutting down trees

marine
to do with the ocean

mining
digging in the earth for things such as coal

plantations
large farms where crops are grown

polar regions
the areas on Earth known as the poles

pollution
dangerous or dirty substances in the air, water, or land

species
a group of animals or plants that are alike

surface
the top, or outer, layer of something

survive
to live

supply
goods, amounts of something

Index